The Regenerative Career Guide

Pathways to an Abundant Future

Matt Powers

This book wouldn't have been possible without the generous donations of hundreds of crowdfunders, help from dozens of generous experts and professionals, and support from several helpful organizations, my friends, my boys, and my wife. Thank you to all who have supported my work, this book, and the regenerative and permaculture movement!

-MP

Front & Back Cover Design: Matt Powers
Front Cover Photo Credit: Raleigh Latham (top left), Matt Powers (top right), Hilary Kearney (bottom left), & Marco Mazza (bottom right)
Back Cover Image Credit: regrarians.org
Formatting & Layout: Matt Powers
Published by PowersPermaculture123, 2017.
ISBN: 978-0-9977043-8-9

Table of Contents

Welcome to the Regenerative Career Guide

Have you heard of the Regenerative Economy?

It's beyond sustainable, beyond organic, and beyond 'green'. It is the path towards an abundant future for all where natural capital is replenished and our economy is rooted in caring for the earth, its peoples, and all its biodiversity. 'To sustain' means 'to maintain' while 'regenerate' is 'to grow back', and while we are far from the global average canopy height and topsoil depth we once had, we can get back on the path towards regenerating those stable investments of natural capital. If we can work together globally in a concerted effort, we can reverse the trends and restore the earth's biodiversity and ecosystems to their former magnitude. Though it will take several generations of diligent effort, we must start now to take advantage of this opportunity.

The systems upon which we base our economy, society, and civilization are currently unsustainable - from how we eat to how we travel to what we wear to how we keep warm at night - it all has to change. We do not have the luxury of choice or time in this equation - our world is facing drastic climate change due to widespread disruption of the carbon, water, nutrient, mineral, and soil cycles which has led to global degradation of the ecological systems that support all biodiversity. The good news is it can all be regenerated within a relatively short timeframe in contrast to the long history of degradation - even the biodiversity that has been lost can be bred back with time and effort to a degree. We now have the science and tools to drastically change our world by partnering with the most powerful forces on earth: the forces of nature itself. We have a lot to learn from nature in its most wild - it is more complicated than anything found in a laboratory setting.

This guide showcases career paths in the new regenerative economy which is rapidly approaching and liberating people from traditional vocations every day in greater numbers. It is by no means a complete list - this guide seeks to showcase some of the best examples out there. If you desire to help your community and the environment while making a living, you are in luck: that's the future - one of thrilling inspiration, hope, and great promise.

You are invited to an abundant future where you can find a career of your choice or own crafting doing what you love while helping others and the planet,

Matt Powers

Regenerative Farming & Ranching

Are you wanting to farm or ranch but...

Are you worried that current practices are unsustainable or not profitable? You're right to be worried. Current standard accepted farming and ranching methods *are* unsustainable and will be surpassed by competitive regenerative systems - many of which are just entering the market now. Farmers and ranchers that re-skill can become leaders in an emerging market. Get in early, learn from the cutting edge, learn regenerative agriculture and ranching: the days of soil degradation are over. Your soils and fields can get better every year now even as you make money ranching or growing crops or market vegetables. You don't need to buy constant inputs from offsite or to spray your fields with poisons. We are now arriving at a sophisticated, biological, and ecological approach to both farming and ranching that sequesters carbon, enriches soil, cleans the water and air, and raises nutrient densities and overall health in plants and animals on the farm. The future of farming is here, and it's profitable, proven, exciting, and hopeful.

Careers

- *Regenerative Farming* - Become a leader in the farming industry by embracing soil building, compost, no till methods, cover crops, bacterial and fungal inoculants, and more as you partner with your bioregion. All of America's farmland could be regenerative - join the growing trend to restore our heritage soils & healthy foods.
- *Carbon Farming* - Build soil and earn money doing it via the carbon credit economy which is spreading and maturing all over the world right now. Some farmers are just focusing on building soil and no longer even sell produce! Carbon farming can be accomplished through ranching or regenerative farming - the choice is yours!
- *Market Gardening* - This can happen anywhere these days near large populations and be very lucrative. Examples like Jean-Martin Fortier and Curtis Stone are proof that profitable businesses are possible in a beyond organic setting on small parcels of land - even in small urban plots of land! Grow HUGE amounts of food in a small area with proven market gardening methods!
- *Holistically Managed Grazing* - Sequester carbon while improving the soil and animal health by mimicking natural patterns of grazing. Make your pastures greener, soil richer, and your calves fatter every year through holistic management. Whether for fiber or meat, this model is spreading like wildfire as ranchers see real results and payoff - consumers want higher quality meat, fat, and fiber, and now there's a regenerative way to deliver it!
- *Pasture Cropping* - A practice blending several disciplines: build soils in a no-till system where grazing animals are used strategically to prepare areas for field crops which are planted in among the native pasture species and harvested mechanically - the grazing animals return to pasture again to clear up the standing biomass and prepare the area for planting again. This allows for pastured animals, field crops, and native plants to share the same space in an elegant syntropic orchestration that while requiring timing gives a much greater yield overall.

EDUCATION

- **The Savory Institute** - Founded by <u>Holistic Management</u> author, Alan Savory, the Savory Institute trains farmers and ranchers in holistic management and even has an accredited professional development track for those looking to teach and consult. <u>Savory.Global/network/#applications</u>
- **Holistic Management International** - This organization gives farmers and ranchers key insights and tools to understand their site, so they can mimic what nature would do. Whether for your social, business, or ecological considerations, holistic management systems provide clarity in decision making, and Holistic Management International offers many educational programs in these areas - some even have FSA Approval. <u>HolisticManagement.org</u>
- **Regenerative Studies, California State Polytechnic University (Pomona)** - With USDA endorsed undergraduate & masters offerings, Cal Poly boasts one of the largest environmental design programs in the country covering everything from urban and regional planning to sustainable architecture to regenerative farming and ecological restoration. <u>Nal.USDA.gov/afsic/edtr/categories/regenerative-farming</u>
- **Polyface Farms Master Program & Summer Internship** - Learn from the leading regenerative ranching example in the USA on the Salatin Family Farm in Virginia. The 5-month summer internship can lead to a year-long Polyface Master Program which can lead to becoming a self-employed entrepreneur, owning and running your own operation or farm, under the Polyface umbrella. <u>PolyfaceFarms.com/apprenticeship/</u>

"Healing the environment while producing nutrient dense life-respecting food is as sacred a task as anyone can imagine. The farming vocation offers all of that and more if the protocols used respect nature's template and nest into local economies and social fabric. Unfortunately, for too long agricultural orthodoxy has not respected nature's patterns, community social fabric, nutrient density, or ecological healing. That trajectory can and should change in the next generation.

By marrying the best of respectful technology with the most primal patterns of animal and plant symbiosis, today's regenerative farmers can do sacred work while being handsomely compensated. It will look nothing like industrial single-species chemical-bathed life-adulterating systems. Healing farms are aesthetically and aromatically sensually romantic. Tapping into the caring portion of the population, these farmers find customer cheerleaders and entrepreneurial opportunity unprecedented in human history.

Lest anyone think this is pie-in-the-sky thinking, I've written 12 books to elucidate these concepts. All of these texts come directly out of my own farming experience at Polyface Farm in Virginia's Shenandoah Valley. Visit us if you don't believe it. Every morning I step out into a marvelous physical expression of provision and abundance. To watch the soil build, earthworms multiply, honey bees proliferate, wildlife increase and food and fiber grow healthy and strong soothes the soul and pays rich spiritual and emotional dividends. And I earn a white collar salary. You should try it."

Joel Salatin
Polyface Farm
Editor, The Stockman Grass Farmer

Agroforestry & Horticulture

Are you a budding orchardist or drawn to the forest?

Our forests are shrinking, and many areas are watching their generational orchards be turned into tract housing - those who love and want to work with trees and forest systems are needed now! Be part of the new generation of orchardists who will move in and regeneratively flip waning conventional orchards into thriving and profitable ecosystems. As more consumers begin to examine and test their food critically, the shift to products strictly from truly regenerative systems will only increase simply because the benefits are verifiable & repeatable - just look to Atsas Organic Farm's example in Cyprus where "in the worst conditions, this olive grove offers the best olive oil [in the world]" (HuffPost, 2017). You can set world records with your produce by partnering with nature too.

The American West and most areas experiencing widespread desertification face wildfires that grow in intensity and destructive nature with each passing year - signaling an ever increasing need for regenerative forest practices, regenerative education, and new levels of forest management, biodiversity support, and vigilance. Degraded and fire-prone areas worldwide are in dire need of experts in forest management - you could be the one to reforest a desert, end the destructive cycle of catastrophic wildfires, bring back the rains to a parched region of the world, or restore the habitat of an nearly extinct animal or plant.

Careers

- *Perennial Farming* - Become a regenerative perennial farmer, sequester carbon by design, build soils, support biodiversity, and grow food, fiber, fuel, and medicine in a system that only improves with age. You can grow herbs, nuts, fruit, oil crops, and more - many of our heirloom staple crops are ripe for reintroduction in a market that values essential oils, variety, and newness.
- *Silvopasture* - Embrace both perennials and grazing animals in an edge system of high productivity and flexibility, with silvopasture's mix of pastures and trees. With so many options, silvopasture systems can rented out to visiting grazing operations or host a diverse variety of unique combinations of animals and plants. You can manage a system that imitates a true wild ecosystem with both plants and animals.
- *Orchard Permaculture* - Managing your orchards like an ecosystem can be incredibly rewarding and profitable as you partner with birds and insects of all kinds in a symphony of biodiversity and abundance.
- *Agroforestry* - Mixing forestry with regenerative agriculture is also possible - many of these systems can be found 'stacked' on one site. You can have grazing, orchard crop, perennial, and annual systems all on one site: you are only limited by your imagination.

EDUCATION

- **The Permaculture Orchard: Beyond Organic** (DVD) - Featuring Stefan Sobkowiak and Miracle Farms, this documentary dives deep into how Stefan designed, installed, and manages his amazing permaculture orchard in Quebec, Canada. It is a beautiful masterpiece showcasing a vibrant example of natural abundance. Get your copy today: PermacultureOrchard.com/shop/
- **Restoration Agriculture Design's Agroforestry & Farm Training** - Online & on-site, RAD offers an array of training for large-scale regenerative farming and agroforestry design and management featuring Mark Shepherd and a diverse team of experts: RestorationAg.com/#training
- **Regenerative Studies, California State Polytechnic University (Pomona)** - With one of the largest regenerative undergraduate & masters programs in the United States, this program covers a broad spectrum of career paths in regeneration. It is also endorsed by the USDA and featured on their website: Nal.usda.gov/afsic/edtr/categories/regenerative-farming
- **Badgersett Research Corporation** - Badgersett has been working on shifting our food system to rely upon woody agriculture staple foods as opposed to annual staples. Instead of wheat, soy, corn, and rice, Badgersett focuses on hazelnuts, hickory-pecans, chestnuts, and hazel hybrids - you can source their genetics directly from their catalog, order one of their Woody Agriculture courses, or join them for a learning field day at their site in Minnesota, USA. Badgersett.com/learning

Badgersett
RESEARCH CORPORATION

RAD™ RESTORATION AGRICULTURE DEVELOPMENT

"Its somewhat poignant that the Regenerative Agriculture & Living movement is growing incrementally and at a pace that is in keeping with its ecological roots. Regenerative agriculture has caught the attention of a whole new generation of producers, entrepreneurs and consumers, many of whom have not come from agricultural backgrounds – bringing a new energy, experience, skills and set of hopes for the future.

Its also pedagogically rich with leading organizations such as the Savory Institute, Holistic Management International, RCS, La Mierda de Vaca, and Regrarians continuously running a diverse array of vocational programs. Supporting these are many regenerative farmers opening their paddocks to all manner of new producers who are eager to produce whilst feasibly regenerating their landscapes, enterprises, communities, watersheds, and soils.

Writers such as the regenerative farmer and academic Charlie Massy are capturing the many great stories out there; Joel Salatin, Greg Judy, Matt Powers, and the Quivera Coalition showing the ways, whilst social media is awash with any number of producers and activists demonstrating the functional beauty of their workplace and production systems.

The data to support regenerative agriculture is coming in too – LandStream's Abe Collins and John Norman are leading that front, whilst apps like Maia Grazing and others continue to build the tech. On the investment front Propagate Ventures and Sustainable Land Management Partners are leading the way to fund innovative projects whose output is regenerative on a whole range of levels.

The greatest distinction between the Regenerative Agriculture & Living movement and those before it is its collegiality and symbiosis – a hallmark of the ecosystems upon which this beautiful world operates and we will all need to foster in order to continue and thrive.

Regrarians is proud to be one of the leading organizations in this space and looks forward to building on its 25 years of service in providing practical training, materials, support and media whilst working closely with other players who are part of the regenerative future."

Lisa Heenan, Isaebella Doherty, & Darren J. Doherty
Directors, Regrarians Ltd.
www.Regrarians.org • www.REX.farm

Soil Analysis & Soil Building

Do you see your future in soils?

The key to regenerating degraded farmland, restoring balance to atmospheric carbon levels, reversing the acidification of the oceans, healthier foods, healthier people, and thriving economies is building healthy soil. We've been degrading and depleting our natural reserves of living topsoil all over the earth where humans have relied upon agriculture for over 10,000 years, even leaving manmade deserts in our wake. Understanding how soil is created allows anyone to restore large and small landscapes alike in an extremely short period of time.

Transform pollution and waste streams into productive soil production systems. Dig deep into the science of remediation by partnering with microscopic soil life to help communities and environments heal. You can make the difference in areas where degradation has been accepted as irreversible - *you can be the change*. Whether you are sourcing the science behind Korean Natural Farming, Bokashi, EM, or Biological Farming, soil life is the cutting edge for all growing operations - no matter the size and scope. With just the humble soil, you can make an incredible difference - **let's dig in!**

Careers

- *Compost Production* - Compost is critical to building soil, sequestering carbon, bringing in soil life, and having a healthy garden or farm. As farmers and ranchers embrace regenerative organic standards, the need for increasingly higher quality compost with specific populations of soil life will rise dramatically as their effectiveness is recognized more widely. Conventional farms can be remediated and transformed rapidly through compost application and incorporation. Compost tea & extract production can make compost production even more profitable, allowing farmers to use their conventional equipment with inputs of liquid compost teas and extracts.
- *Soil Life Production* - EM, Bokashi, Korean Natural Farming, Biological Farming and more emerging practices focus on promoting specific populations of soil life for higher quality products and for targeting specific problems or situations. So little is known about soil life that new discoveries, insights, and methods are constantly emerging, making soil life production one of the most exciting areas to be involved with. Bioremediation of the most toxic and damaged soils, unlocking soil nutrients to save an entire harvest, battling infamous pathogens and pests, and gaining the highest yields, nutrient densities, and levels of medicinal compounds can be achieved through specific partnerships with focused populations of soil life.
- *Soil Testing Laboratory & Consultation* - Along with more sophisticated soil building and soil life generating practices, advanced soil testing methods have arrived, but few are trained in the microscopy needed.

Education

- **Dr. Elaine Ingham's Soil Food Web Inc.** - Featuring everything from soil life identification to microscopy to composting professionally, this series of courses and soil food web certification are the regenerative industry standard of excellence in soil science. Taught by USDA Soil Primer author and world famous soil scientist, Dr. Elaine Ingham, this program will give you the ability to dramatically transform landscapes, make the best compost and compost teas, troubleshoot real-life soil problems, start your own soil laboratory, and become a professional soil consultant. Learn from the woman who's Phd was based on coming up with a simple and clear methodology for testing the soil foodweb populations from a living system! SoilFoodWeb.com

- **Ohio State University's Soil Science Undergraduate & Graduate Programs** - The OSU soil programs are in the School of Environment and Natural Resources (SENR) where graduate students learn the practice and methodologies of modern soil science as they study current research and discuss their insights with experts like distinguished professor Dr. Rattan Lal, one of the leading experts in soil science and carbon sequestration Senr.osu.edu/graduate/soil-science

- **Cornell University's Graduate Field of Soil and Crop Sciences** - An esteemed and established program that has adopted regenerative practices increasingly and leads to Phd, MPS, & MS programs. It has a focus on agronomy, soil science, crop science, and environmental science. Scs.cals.cornell.edu/graduate

THE OHIO STATE UNIVERSITY

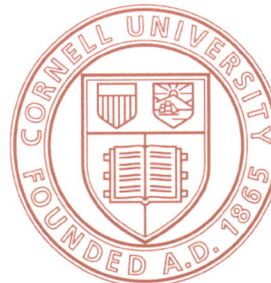

Cornell University

9

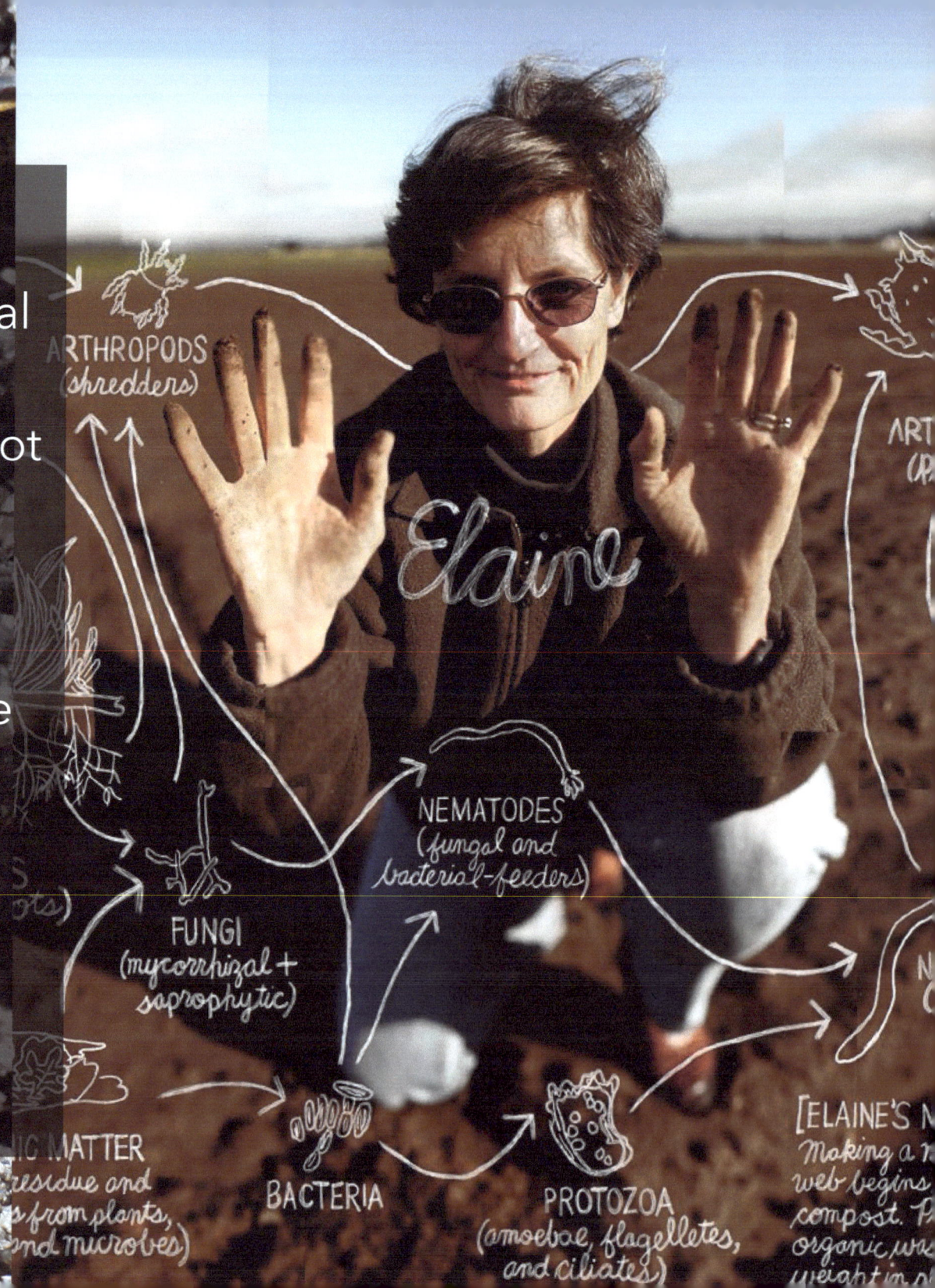

"There are more microbial cells in your body than cells of yourself. We've got to get this incredible knowledge out to everybody about how dependent we are on the web that we live in. Everything's connected."

Dr. Elaine Ingham Phd.
author, soil scientist, researcher, & biological farmer
SoilFoodWeb.com

Mycology &
Fungi Cultivation

Are fungi fascinating you?

Perhaps the fastest growing and one of the most profitable industries in the regenerative economy, fungi farming is capturing the imaginations of many as they see what prices shiitakes and other fungal delicacies get in the market and how easy they are to cultivate. Additionally, medicinal mushrooms have recently seized the spotlight - making strides with FDA testing for cancer treatment and even patents for neural regeneration. Recent discoveries in fungi are also breaking down our understanding of taxonomy and the origins of life on earth itself. Humans, all animals, and all plants are all part and partner with fungi - it is an inescapable thread to our reality that is why it is so shocking that Mycology as a branch of scientific study is less than 100 years old! We only cultivate a small group of mushrooms though we partner with a wide diversity of fungi - including the more familiar yeasts and molds. Though Asia has long used mushrooms medicinally, the West is finally catching up just as interest and demand is sparking. You can grow fungal medicines, gourmet mushrooms, remediate toxins from soils, brew probiotic drinks, or break down excess waste - *All with Fungi!*

Careers

- *Fungi Farmer* - Farmers are needed to grow gourmet mushrooms, medicinal mushrooms, mycelium in bulk, and mycorrhizal inoculants for other farmers. You can grow mushrooms that fight cancer or are served at local restaurants. You can help others grow their own mushrooms or improve their farm.
- *Fungi Fiber & Dye* - Faux leather, fireproof building materials, dyes, paints, and more - fungi are incredibly diverse in their expression both in life and in preservation. We are discovering new applications every day for fungi, and it is opening doors to regenerative niches constantly.
- *Mycoremediation* - Fungi are nature's most talented and creative chemists - they can remove, rearrange, and embody many heavy metals and toxins of all kinds. Remediating soils and water often relies upon fungi even when using plants in an ecosystemic remediation design. You can work with fungi and heal the earth and get paid to do it. Many communities facing serious environmental toxins don't know about the new solutions they can source and just need local businesses to help - you can be that presence!
- *Nutritionists & Medical Practitioners with a Fungal Focus* - Partner with fungi in your medical or nutritional consultations. While Asian medicine has long led the way with medicinal mushrooms, current research leaves no room of doubt: mushrooms and fungi provide medicinal compounds unlike any other source and they can be cultivated at home inexpensively. Help patients get the treatment they can afford and thrive on!
- *Breweries* - All over the world in almost all cultures, fermentations of all sorts have been made partnering with yeast and other microbes to make alcohol and probiotic drinks.

Education

- ***MycoLogos, School of Mycology*** - The first mycology school EVER! Serving students of all levels of expertise both in-person and online, this Portland, Oregon based school will provide critical teaching and training that cannot be found anywhere else in the world. Led by author, educator, and entrepreneur, Peter McCoy of Radical Mycology, this school will provide professional development and mastery level courses as well as introductory training and education in fungi through a diversity of contexts and career paths.
- **Golden Coast Mead** - Learn with dry mead creator and Golden Coast Mead founder, Frank Golbeck, in person at his Meadery or through online courses starting in 2018. Frank has helped start 5 successful meaderies, each under different owners, in the San Diego area and plans on spreading the magic of dry mead to fermentation connoisseurs everywhere! See what yeast can do with regenerative sources - you can heal large-landscapes partnering with bees and native plants. Learn how with Frank Golbeck! GoldenCoastMead.com

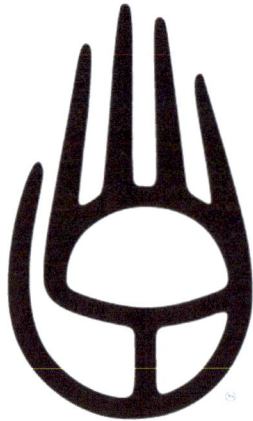

MYCOLOGOS

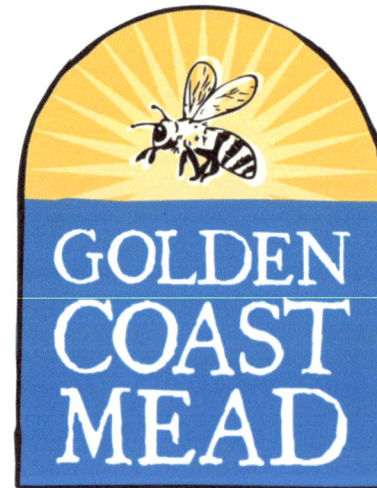

GOLDEN COAST MEAD

"One of the most rapidly developing fields in permaculture is applied mycology. From improving food production and resource management, to increasing soil fertility and helping cleanup pollution, it seems that humans have only just begun to recognize the important roles that mushrooms and other fungi offer for enhancing holistic designs. Fungi are some of our greatest teachers on nature's principles and patterns – archetypal permaculturalists that are often found at the center of any ecological web, guiding its succession and long-term health. By learning to work with fungi and effectively apply them in your design practice, you will be on the cutting edge of this fascinating and endlessly regenerative aspect of permaculture. The future truly is Fungi. Join the mycocultural revolution!"

Peter McCoy
author, mycologist, permaculturist, and educator.
Mycologos.world & RadicalMycology.com

Beekeeping & Vermiculture

Sweet on bees or curious about worms?

Partnering with bees and worms has never been as profitable. High-end dry mead is taking the market by storm and creating a demand for higher quality honey at a higher price, and worms of all kinds are being used to recycle waste and enrich garden, ranch, and farm soils. Beyond bees and worms, other insects are now entering into the market and disrupting previously fixed feed to egg ratios in chicken operations, styrofoam recycling, and organic farming and gardening solutions. Bees also open up a great deal of possibilities including pollination, wax production, and medicinal qualities of honey and pollen. Land can be regenerated partnering with these small creatures who do so much in the environment around us.

Careers:

- *Honey, Beeswax, & Pollen Production* - Perhaps the sweetest endeavor of them all - honey production leads to limitless value added products that are well-loved and increasingly in demand as a natural sweetener. Regenerating a landscape to produce high quality honey is a lower ceiling to entry than most farming endeavors involving land. The byproducts of honey production: wax and pollen are also incredible in their own applications. Become a Beekeeper and be a regenerative steward over your hives and land.
- *Beekeeping Services* - Tend farmers', home owners', and orchardists' pollinators for them - arrangements range from the site keeping all the honey, being part of a CSA, or taking none of it, leaving it all to you - they may value the pollination of their orchards over any honey at all!
- *Worm Farming* - Raise worms to supply to farmers, ranchers, home gardeners, and compost operations.
- *Bioremediation & Recycling with Worms* - Mealworms can eat styrofoam and transform it in their digestion back into compostable organic matter. Earthworms can help recycle paper and cardboard waste as well. Teams of worms and insects can break down complex mixtures in-situ that are too hard to remove, filter, and process.
- *Vermicomposting* - Composting agricultural and municipal waste can provide incredible byproducts that are valuable to farmers, gardeners, landscapers, and more. The future of municipal waste will be rooted in partnerships with earthworms of all kinds.
- *Black Soldier Fly Larvae & Other Insects for Animal Feed* - Worms and larvae of all kinds are used as animal feed because they are incredibly high in protein. Some companies even sell kits to produce insects for animal feed at home! For chickens, it is an incredible protein source that lowers feed costs immensely! You can scale up and serve your area's need for alternative feed solutions!

Education

- ***Vermicomposting Course with Living Earth Ecology*** - Eddy Garcia and his team teach vermicomposting along with a series of regenerative online courses. Eddy Garcia discovered mealworms digest styrofoam over a year before Stanford University published their studies on them, and he has developed a method to turn styrofoam into rich soil. Eddy teaches several other courses as well on soil, natural swimming pools, aquaculture, and more. LivingEarthSystems.com

- ***Bee College in Cheyenne at the LCCC extension*** - A Bee Friendly Company's Michael Jordan teaches courses at the University of Wyoming. Michael has traveled the world studying different beekeeping methods, and he teaches beekeeping extensively online via PermaEthos, in-person, and at University of Wyoming. Michael is a connoisseur of beekeeping and loves learning and sharing as much as he can - for that reason, he understands and teaches a wide-range of beekeeping styles, techniques, and philosophies.

- ***Girl Next Door Honey Bee Classes*** - Hilary Kearney hosts online and in-person beekeeping classes in San Diego, California from an organic, regenerative perspective. Her online courses range from introductory to advanced, focusing on everything from honey harvesting to swarm removal. Start your beekeeping adventure and work with a hive in your backyard this year! GirlNextDoorHoney.com/

- **Beekeeping Online** - In only three courses, go from introduction to certification: become a Master Beekeeper from home! Through the University of Montana and taught by lead bee researchers, this program is endorsed by the Montana State Beekeepers Association and The American Honey Producers Association. Umt.edu/sell/programs/bee/

"The average beekeeper age is 57. So, there is a definite need for a new generation of beekeepers. Beekeepers are facing more challenges than ever but have been slow to consider their own role in the problem. New beekeepers have the chance to change the unsustainable aspects of the system. It has been really exciting to see my peers pioneer this shift. They are putting the needs of their bees first and coming up with creative new business models. Get started keeping bees and find out where you might fit in the movement."

Hilary Kearney

beekeeper, entrepreneur, and educator.
GirlNextDoorHoney.com

GIRL
NEXT DOOR
HONEY

Hilary Kearney 2017.

Natural Fiber & the Fibershed

Do you love working with animals or natural fiber?

Have you heard of the Fibershed? It's an incredible organization based upon a soil to soil bioregional concept of fiber production and distribution. It's the primary way natural fibers were cultivated and used throughout human history - only since the advent of petrochemical clothing and its environmentally catastrophic consequences did we move away from this. Natural fiber based clothing and textiles solve many problems inherent in conventional synthetic fiber: microfiber pollution in the ocean is out of control with no clear solution in the near future, and toxic clothing and textiles are poisoning our bodies and environment through everyday use. The Fibershed highlights a path of beauty and natural harmony - one of rich heritage, beauty, utility, and cultural value.

Whether raising animals for meat or for fiber, a holistic approach is needed to regenerate and preserve landscapes all over the world. Overgrazing has been and continues to be responsible for desertification in many regions. We need ranchers and all owners of grazing animals to rotate their animals constantly to regenerate the landscape - this requires new thinking, retooling, and young and able-bodied people to join the ranks and start making this happen everywhere! Join the Fibershed movement & start a soil to soil fibershed system in your area!

Careers

- **Natural Fiber Farming** - Jute, hemp, nettle, flax, cotton, and more are making a resurgence in the market as consumers become conscious of animal welfare and synthetic contaminants. These vigorous crops and an eager market are just waiting for someone to grow them regeneratively!
- **Natural Fiber Animals** - Fleece, wool, mohair, and more - sustainable animal fibers are durable, unique, regenerative, and timeless. If you love animals and their fiber, this is an undeniable win-win!
- **Fiber Processing** - Natural fibers need to be cleaned and processed before they can be spun, knit, sewn, or woven. Every bioregion needs machine-minded individuals to design and run processing facilities for a huge spectrum of fiber sources with specific requirements.
- **Natural Dyes** - Gardeners, wilderness foragers, mushroom cultivators, and more can participate in the dye and ink market. Many of the most vibrant natural dyes still come from plant sources like true indigo blue. If you are looking for guilt-free, dazzling colors, you might love developing and selling natural dyes.
- **Local Textile Producers** - Local designers & fabricators are needed to take locally processed and raised fiber and refine it into products to sell in the market. We need local fashion, small-scale textile operations, and designers everywhere who source alternative energy and return their valuable waste to the soil in their biome.

Education

- **Traditional Indigenous Systems** - All over the world, indigenous peoples have handed down natural fiber systems for generations beyond written memory, and we can still learn from their example today. In your area, there are indigenous teachers with information that can help you give back as you get back to basics by partnering with nature using proven patterns and ethical systems.
- **Fibershed** - This amazing organization hosts the annual Wool Symposium, workshops, and classes on all aspects of the fibershed system. They are helping communities all over the world reconnect to their local fiber sources and celebrate them. Support & learn from this incredible organization - Take Part in the Fibershed Economy! Fibershed.com
- **Natural Fabric Dyeing: Eco Colour, Print, & Pattern** - A seasonal online introduction to natural dyes using plant sources for prints and making traditional patterns with Justine Aldersey-Williams of The Wild Dyery. Explore the rainbow of possibility with natural dyes: NaturalFabricDyeing.com/study/

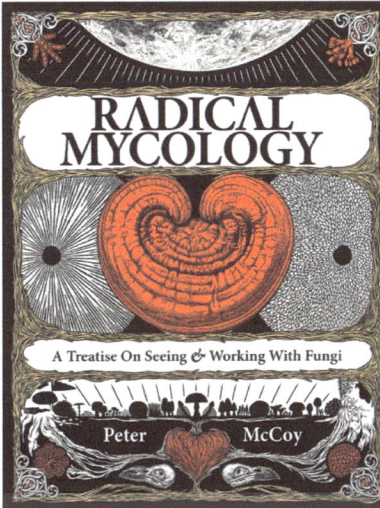

Permatecture, Ecological Engineering, & Alt Energy

Partner with Nature in Power, Building, & Technical Design

You can partner with nature and still be highly technical - in fact, we need a lot more of that in the regenerative space! There is a need for new machines for new and old crops - these have to be made by professional designers and fabricators. New products and industries readily come out of these kinds of creative environments as new technology makes marketable goods profitable to explore. An early leader in the organic movement in the US, Elliot Coleman is widely known for his line of tools designed specifically for the organic market gardener. These tools and machines are in demand - we just need more engineers, builders, and designers to meet that demand. New designers are also needed for large-scale projects including alternative energy, architecture, and water harvesting.

Design homes that are completely off the grid - or even better, design homes that power the grid itself! Water harvesting and purifying and managing our waste at home has to come easily, and new engineering minds are needed to create a future that partners with nature inside and outside the home in all settings ranging from the rural to the urban. New and old technologies are all being considered as our civilization considers a world without fossil fuel reliance.

Careers

- *Permatecture* - Build with natural materials using regenerative local inputs and ethical labor - be a leading local example of regenerative architecture. Design homes that heat and cool themselves passively, harvest and purify their own water, have natural swimming pools, have indoor greenhouses, compost all their waste, clean their own gray and black water on-site, and much more. Beyond LEED is Permatecture!
- *Ecological Engineering* - Almost everything needs to be reimagined from a new regenerative perspective. Our one-time-use culture is coming to a crashing halt - we needed to fill the gap it will leave. You can take part in shaping the world to come by being a regenerative engineer - partner with nature & design a world beyond current understanding. With the advent of such advances as nanoclay, industrial trompes, drones, and automation, we can now do what was impossible only a few years ago. Our cities, our homes, our toilets, our municipal waste, water treatment, and everything in between can be improved with your contribution - be part of this sea change in our culture.
- *Alternative Energy* - Solar, Wind, Hydrological, Pneumatic, GeoThermal, Biodigestion, & Human Power - the technologies rising to meet the challenge of a world beyond fossil fuels are abundant and exciting. It is a thrilling opportunity to improve how we all live our daily lives - you can help make this huge step easier!

Education

- **Renewable Energy Engineering Degree** - Oregon Tech offers the first North American renewable energy 4 year bachelor's program! This incredible flagship program is perfect for those serious about being a leader in the future of energy. Oit.edu/academics/degrees/renewable-energy-engineering

- **Energy & Clean Technology MBA** - Berkeley Haas offers a celebrated, full-time MBA program that blends engineering, environmental science, renewable energy, and clean tech with regular annual events, organizations, and gatherings to support and facilitate career development. Mba.haas.berkeley.edu/academics/energy.html

- **Environment & Sustainability Minor** - Known to engineers everywhere as the standard in excellence, MIT also has an academic track for engineers wanting to focus on the environment and designing for the future. Sustainability.mit.edu/study-classroom-opportunities-students

- **Eldenbridge** - Learn permaculture from an engineer's perspective with Alan Booker in Huntsville, Alabama. Classes range from traditional permaculture to more technical aspects like drones and mapping technologies. Eldenbridge.org/classes-and-events/

- **Sustainable Energy Systems Engineering Phd Program** - This incredible program from Texas A&M University-Kingsville focuses on facing the future with sustainably and regeneratively powered solutions. Get your Phd in sustainable energy systems & design the future! Tamuk.edu/engineering/SESE/

- **CalEarth** - Take a course or become an apprentice with the California Institute of Earth Architecture. Learn about Superadobe and how we can we can all safely participate in building our homes and community structures using natural building materials. CalEarth.org

"The decisions being made today by engineers, architects, and other design professionals will determine whether our cities are the kind of place we want to live in the future. The problem is that most of the design approaches currently being taught and practiced were not created with long-term consequences in mind and have resulted in many of our human landscapes being unhealthy and unsustainable.

But the entire field of design is now undergoing a massive transformation as people are beginning to demand healthy and regenerative places to live and work. Communities designed around access to nutrient dense food, green buildings, clean energy, and natural landscapes will be the ones poised to be the most successful in this new environment.

Some of the biggest challenges and opportunities of the coming decades will involve fundamentally redesigning the systems that support our civilization, moving them away from their current consumptive and extractive models, and toward designs modeled on natural systems that are more productive and abundant. The most in-demand designers over the next few years will be those who are trained to help build this regenerative future."

Alan Booker

executive director and lead teacher at Eldenbridge Institute,
Eldenbridge.org

Eldenbridge
INSTITUTE

Alternative Transportation

What comes after Combustion Engines?

We are about to witness pedal-based vehicles, solar-powered planes, and alternative transportation of all kinds fill the air and roadways around us in the cities, farms, and everywhere between. Just as it took over a thousand designs to arrive at a superior automobile model, it will take another technological revolution to fill the gap left by fossil fuel usage once it is fully phased out. Making these technologies more open-source, easy to maintain and repair at home, and accessible to all will do more than just decentralize control over transportation, but switching to something like pedal-powered vehicles will increase overall health, lower healthcare costs, lower accident rates, lower mortality rates, empower drivers to maintain their own vehicles, & lower emission rates dramatically. New designs are needed on a mass scale from drones to buses to boats to family cars - you could invent the Model-T of the regenerative transportation age!

Careers

- *Electric Vehicle Design & Fabrication* - Though Tesla grabs headlines, the entire car industry has its eye on the future as well. Inventors, engineers, skilled craftsmen, and researchers are needed to design, build, and test prototypes for what will become the car, truck, or municipal transportation of tomorrow - the race is on.
- *Alternative Fuel Vehicle Conversion & Design* - Converting the existing fleet of vehicles to alternative regenerative fuel sources or a hybrid of electric and alternative fuel will save energy and resources, and it will prevent an enormous amount of waste. With the multiplicity of engines and car designs already in place, it will require an equally detailed response to the problem: the need for courageous designers is incalculable!
- *Alternative Public Transit* - Our trains, buses, trolleys, subways, and more need to be retrofitted or redesigned altogether - we now know so much more. Many cities are already embracing emission free public transit - it's becoming increasingly popular as demand continues to rise. Rethink the way your city moves people!
- *Foot Pedal Vehicles* - "Bicycle Cars" are another potential future that has incredible merit. It's the healthiest option for everyone - less accidents, slower speeds, more control, more repairability within the car owner's range, & greater health. These designs will completely displace the fuel-based paradigm and embrace a healthful alternative path.
- *Solar Planes, Drones, & Gliders* - The demand for a drone-based delivery system is high but designers & operators are needed. Solar planes and gliders are also showing great promise, but both are still in the early days of knowing what's possible. The first nonstop flight around the world in a solar plane only recently occurred.

Education

- **Solar Car Project** - Considered America's best solar car program and internationally ranked, University of Michigan leads with a serious focus on solar transportation, nearing two decades of sustained leadership. If you are interested in designing with a team of enthusiastic and committed like-minded engineers, look into this program. Solarcar.Engin.umich.edu

- **ASME Human Powered Vehicle Challenge** - The American Society of Mechanical Engineers (ASME) chapter at Ohio Northern University has been working on a pedal powered vehicle for over two years and has gained some recognition for it, but you can join ASME and take part in this challenge from anywhere - you only have to be enrolled in an engineering program and be part of ASME! Start the Challenge at your school! Asme.org/events/competitions/human-powered-vehicle-challenge-(hpvc)

- **American Solar Challenge** - A distance race across the US using only sunlight to power the vehicles, this race is one that collegiate level student teams can take part in from around the world. Ready to race with the sun? AmericanSolarChallenge.org/about/american-solar-challenge/

- **Electric Drivetrain Technology** - The University of Colorado Boulder and the University of Colorado Colorado Springs's graduate programs together provide a graduate certificate program to enhance a masters degree with a focus on cutting-edge, professional automative technologies. Colorado.edu/graduateschool/distance-education/certificate-programs/electric-drivetrain-technology

LEARN FROM
THE WORLD'S TOP
REGENERATIVE SYSTEM
DESIGNERS
INSPIRATION AND KNOWLEDGE
IN AN UNCERTAIN FUTURE.
WWW.SUSTAINABLEDESIGNMASTERCLASS.COM

Food
& Beverage

Do you crave the best in food and drink?

The science is in: the best foods are hyperlocal, regeneratively grown in living soils, perennial, native, and seasonal. Indigenous traditions lead the way with indigenous recipes, plants, and techniques. To top it off, you can now learn directly from indigenous chefs, leaders in the seed to table culinary movement, and adventurous chefs from all schools adopting new heirloom and traditional ingredients. The palette with which a chef can work with is now diverse and broad ranging.

Foraged foods, wild foods, and new foods of all kinds especially in the world of fermentation are being welcomed onto plates all over the world. After years of seeing the adventurous chefs in our media dream up new recipes and techniques, consumers are wanting new flavors, textures, and colors. Partnering with nature is always going to lead to innovation, the most vivid flavors, and the highest nutrient densities - a sure foundation for a rewarding career in culinary arts especially as consumers need healthier foods that support their local environment.

Careers

- *Indigenous Chefs* - As indigenous food systems education becomes more widely available through organizations like NATIFS, more opportunities will be available to become a chef focused on indigenous ingredients and methods to meet the huge demand for authentic indigenous foods. Though people all over the world celebrate cuisine and culture, there are at the same time hundreds and thousands of indigenous cultural traditions being neglected that are waiting to create a new sensation and broaden our understanding of food, health, the earth, all life, and culture.
- *Seed to Table Restaurants* - While farm to table restaurants are increasingly common, the next stage is to focus further up the genetic chain of events and have food only grown from locally adapted seeds for the best possible food. It's not just local - it's rooted in the history of the local area, just like the people living there. Become a deep part of your community by starting your area's first seed to table restaurant!
- *Foraging* - Many don't realize that their wild mushrooms imply foraging, but they certainly do! As more wild foods are experienced, the higher the demand will become. Foragers will be needed! Do you like to get lost in the forest while hunting for hidden edible gems? Become a Forager!

TheSiouxChef.com 2017

Education
- ***NATIFS: North American Traditional Indigenous Food Systems*** - This amazing nonprofit organization focuses on spreading North American traditional indigenous food systems education, food access, and research - be part of the North American indigenous renaissance and spread healthy and regenerative foods and practices. Natifs.org
- ***Urban Outdoor Skills*** - Pascal Baudar's school for foraging, wildcrafting, and culinary alchemy features a broad range of wild cuisine blending traditional insights from many different cultures. Learn to see the abundance everywhere with Pascal! UrbanOutdoorSkills.com
- ***Elliot Coleman*** - An early leader in the organic foods movement, his catalog of works teach the foundation of regenerative market gardening and farm-to-table, seasonal cooking, and his suite of tools sold through Johnny's Select Seeds is unparalleled. Pickup one of Eliot's books and you'll be amazed!
- ***The Sioux Chef*** - Ever imagined what it would be like to use indigenous ingredients in a 5-star restaurant setting? That's what Sean Sherman is all about: he creates incredibly beautiful and delicious dishes using only indigenous ingredients and teaches others how to do it too. Learn with Sean, an incredible example and teacher - become an indigenous chef! Sioux-Chef.com

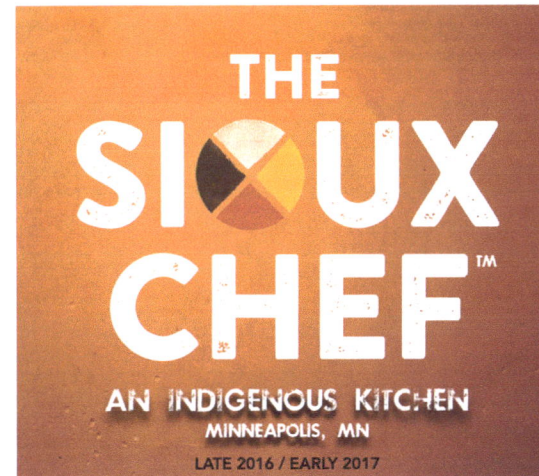

"Why isn't the original indigenous diet all the rage today? It's hyperlocal, ultraseasonal, uberhealthy: no processed foods, no sugar, no wheat (or gluten), no dairy, no high-cholesterol animal products. It's naturally low glycemic, high protein, low salt, plant based with lots of grains, seeds, and nuts. Most of all, it's utterly delicious. It's what so many diets strive to be but fall short for lack of context. This is a diet that connects us all to nature and to each other in the most direct and profound ways."

Sean Sherman

founder of The Sioux Chef & NATIFS
NATIFS.org & Sioux-Chef.com

Medicine & Therapy

Do you want to heal people using Natural Cures?

Do you use essential oils? Kelp? Herbs? Chinese medicine? Naturopathic medicine? Do you juice or make smoothies? More and more doctors, patients, and people in general are realizing *food is our medicine* as Hippocrates wrote over two thousand of years ago. It might be more accurate to say *nature is our medicine* since studies show that immersing ourselves in nature, using wild plants, and living as part of natural cycles enrich and lengthen our lives and our resiliency. In fact, all medicines are derived originally from natural sources and then often synthesized from coal tar or other petroleum-based product. As fossil fuels become more scarce and more damaging in their usage, natural medicines will once again become the medicine of choice.

Naturopathic doctors have begun to source wild and local, native plants for medicinal applications over what they are learning to source in their standard training since local, wild foods have sometimes thousands of times the nutrients or active medicinal compounds in them compared to common store bought foods. Mushrooms both wild and cultivated are also being used increasingly in medicinal applications in the western world - in a mirror to the longstanding tradition in Asia. As the power of nature and food is more fully realized, we'll see a huge shift from conventional medicine to local, regenerative natural therapies and medicines. Join the revolution, and start healing the planet and people at the same time!

Careers

- *Regenerative Nutritionists* - Nutritionists don't have to be an echo of a textbook - they can apply the same principles they learned in their schooling but with wild foods with the same but more abundant or effective medicinal attributes.
- *Regenerative Doctors* - Naturopaths are gaining ground in the medical field because of the high demand for natural cures. You can source regenerative foods and medicines in your medical practice. Learn your area's potent medicinals and how they are used, so you can serve your patients at a higher level. Start a health retreat or a medicinal food forest at your doctor's office or homesite. The future of medicine is found in fertile soil - plant your seeds wisely and become a doctor focused on regenerative solutions.
- *Regenerative Therapist* - Help patients get their lives back on track using the natural world as a source for healing their bodies and minds. Teach people to partner with nature to keep themselves healthy and to heal from trauma.

Education

- **Nutritional Solutions** - Jeanne Wallace Phd is a leading expert in nutritional oncology, yet many don't know that she's relied upon her homesite's food forest for powerful health solutions for almost two decades. Learn from a leader in nutrition focused on regenerative sources - become a health expert that heals the planet too! Nutritional-Solutions.net

- **Thallaso Therapy: The Longevity Revolution** - Learn about thallaso therapy from Antoinette Marquez, owner of AMA Sea Beauty, and its long tradition of healing people in Europe. Part beautification and part therapy, thallaso therapy uses the ocean to heal in a joyful, regenerative, and invigorating way. Forage from the seashore, sequester the lost minerals from land back into the soil and our bodies, and help people heal in a natural, gentle way.

- **Chestnut School for Herbal Medicine** - Learn how to grow, forage, harvest, transform, and store medicinal herbs in this beautiful, clear, and fun online course with a large team of instructors. They'll even dive into how to help you start your own business! Learn with a manual or strictly online - the course structure and breadth is amazing!

Chestnut School of Herbal Medicine

AMA SEABEAUTY™

AMA
SEABEAUTY™

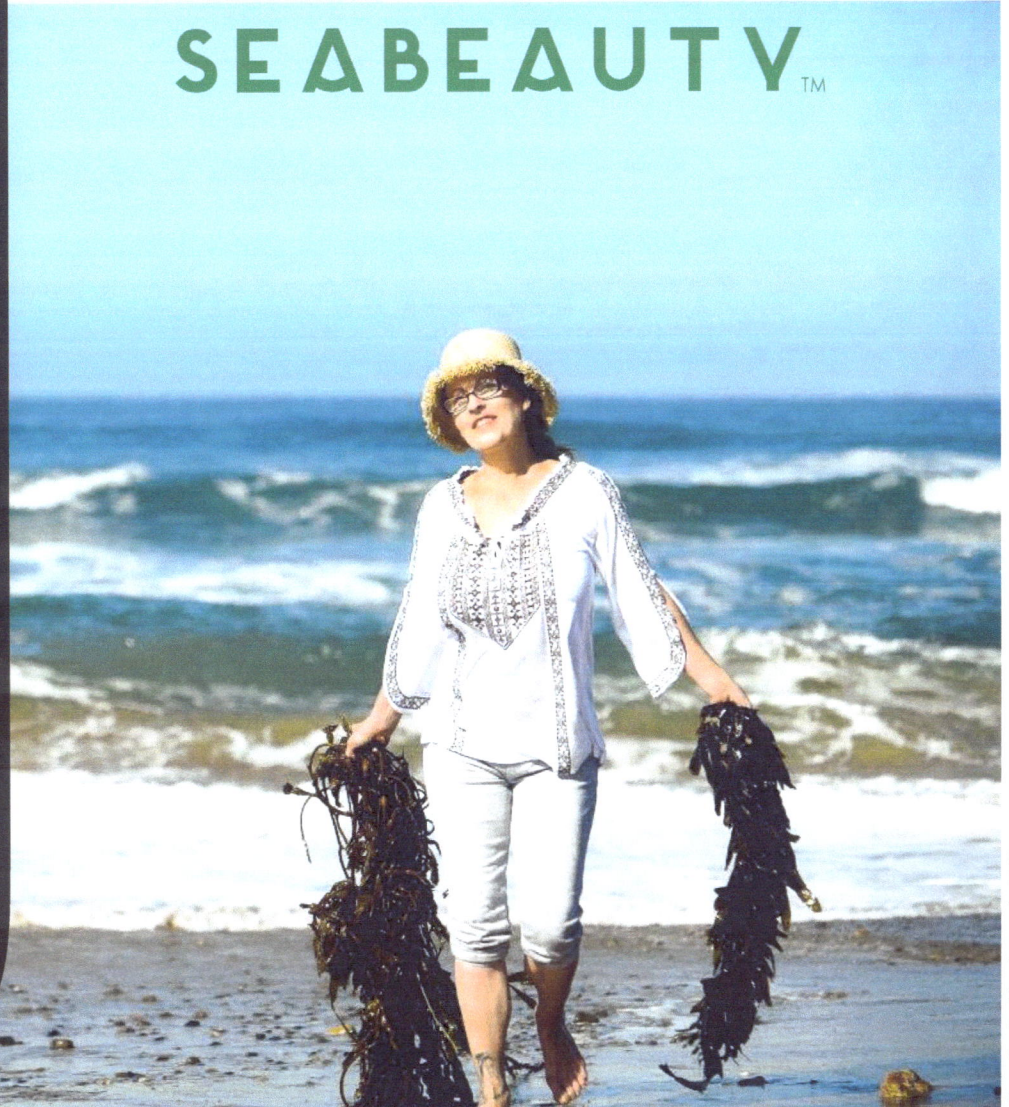

"Foraging or Kelping moves you from a beach goer to a beach participator. Collecting seaweed gets you up close and personal with the sea, its vegetation, and the ocean animals who live in the intertidal zones. Suddenly seaweed doesn't seem intimidating, scary, or gross. When the tide pulls back you have an opportunity to touch, feel, and engage with seaweed in its natural growing environment.

Foraging gives you an opportunity to peek into the homes of seaweed/kelp/algae to see how their gardens grow, how they live their lives and who they hang out with. Becoming a Kelper is perhaps one of the best way to begin ocean stewardship!"

Antoinette Marquez

Co-founder Ama SeaBeauty/Pharmersea,
Thalassotherapist, Kelper, & Author of
The Longevity Revolution
AMASeaBeauty.com

PhotoCredit: Alan Antiporda 2017.

Landscaping & Design

Do you love transforming sites?

Are you always sketching out designs or using your computer to generate your dream site? You can make dreams come true for yourself and others and follow a path of designing regeneratively. Your work and contribution will be invaluable as it enriches the landscape and land owners everywhere you serve. Help others see your vision by honing your skills in graphic design, mapping, drone operation, CAD, GPS technologies, and more.

Not only that - you can help farmers and ranchers make wise decisions that will affect landscapes, lives, and livelihoods for decades if not centuries. Help plan, organize, and design restoration in both commercial and governmental settings. Reimagine and heal large landscapes like the Loess Plateau Project which was a World Bank project along with America and China. There is funding, understanding, and need for this work - you can help and make a living restoring landscapes all over the world. The need to regenerate degraded or damaged areas will only increase as the powerful effects of making these changes becomes more widely recognized.

Careers

- *Ecological Landscaping* - designing & managing regenerative landscapes as a business can be incredibly rewarding both financially and emotionally. Become a 21st century landscaper - embrace regeneration!
- *Permaculture Homestead Consulting & Installation* - Help homeowners get off the grid in style with a permaculture design and installation business - create a team of specialists and start flipping homes into the regenerative future!
- *Regenerative Farm & Ranch Planning* - Help farmers, ranchers, and orchardists transition into the regenerative economy by transforming their business, properties, skill sets, and routines.
- *Large-Scale Land Restoration* - The return on investment in The Loess Plateau Project is setting the stage for a huge focus on large-scale restoration plans for all the areas humans once thrived in. Even deserts like the Sahara can be restored to their rich savannah past, and even cities will need to be rethought and remade. It will take time and investment, and you can you provide the expertise and vision.
- *MapMaking* - Use the latest programs and technology to generate amazing maps - or use your artistic talent to create beautiful renditions of your vision. There is real demand for expertise with CAD, Google Earth Pro, GPS, and Drones - you can provide technical, artistic, and/or computer support for a project that changes our world for the better.

SouthWoods Permaculture 2017.

Education

- **Ecological Landscape Mastery Course** - Permaculture Skill Center's co-founder, Erik Ohlsen, along with a team of guest expert instructors take students on a regenerative educational journey, so they can help transform their community into one of abundance, beauty, functionality, and regeneration by design through landscaping. Erik even has a free video series to introduce the program: ErikOhlsen.com/elm-free-video-series/
- **United Designers** - Expert designer and permaculture educator, Daniel Halsey of Southwoods Permaculture, teaches the United Designers online video course series which focuses on professional site designs that are easy to navigate and use to showcase to clients and the public detailed plans quickly. Daniel's style of mapmaking and design are superb and iconic - there's no better example or teacher on this topic. SouthwoodsCenter.com/design-resources.html
- **REX Online** - The most comprehensive online farm planning program in the world. Darren Doherty and his team of Regrarians have transformed thousands of sites across the globe. Their program is superbly thorough in its approach to site design especially in terms of technical details and tools. It also includes lifetime access, so continually learn and progress with a global community of designers. Plan out a regenerative farm with a proven method rooted in PA Yeomans Scale of Permanence and nuanced with permaculture and dozens of other professional disciplines and methodologies. Darren's lifetime of experience terraforming thousands of farms and landscapes in diverse climates has given him a professional regenerative lens like no other. Rex.farm

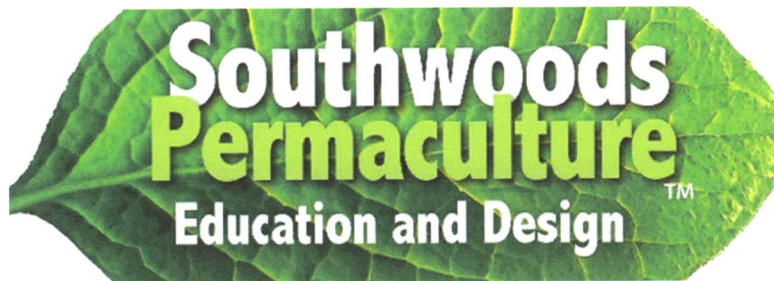

PermacultureSkillsCenter.org

"You can have a meaningful career restoring the planet and make a meaningful income at the same time. I am proof, and I know many others that are doing this right now as a career, and that can be you."

Erik Ohlsen

author, designer, teacher, and co-founder and co-director of the Permaculture Skills Center in Sebastopol, CA.
PermacultureSkillsCenter.org

Regenerative Ocean & Wetland Farming

Want to heal the oceans?

You're not alone - we do too! For a long time, there wasn't a clear path to regeneration in the ocean setting, but that time is over. We now know what we have to do: sequester the excess carbon and nitrogen into biology like kelp and shellfish and then bring it back on land to return it to the soil. We need people who love the ocean to farm it, to help regenerate and restore the damaged shore, wetland, riparian, and reef ecologies, and to protect them from further degradation.

Though we do not yet know how to measure how much of our oxygen comes from ocean phytoplankton exactly, it is clear that half to two thirds of all our atmospheric oxygen is generated through the life cycles of these tiny ocean plants. The health of the ocean is our health, and more and more people are figuring that out and using products from the sea. You can forage and work with the bounty of the ocean, but only if it is a wild and abundant system. We need regenerative farmers, stewards, and businesses to support them and connect them to the consumers on shore who need these products and want to help heal the ocean too. We all can do our part but some of us get to grow new kelp forests - join the regenerative farming movement and start your own forest under the waves!

Careers

- **Regenerative Ocean Farming** - Food, beauty, fertilizer, supplement, & health products of all kinds from the ocean can be regenerative as long as they are taking the excess nutrients that came from the land back onto the land - these leached minerals and nutrients can be from natural sources or conventional farming and ranching practices that destroy habitat and soil. Every shore and river that meets the ocean must be tended and rewilded strategically - you can foster the return of wildness to these areas and turn the problem into a valuable solution.
- **Regenerative Wetland Farming** - Before arriving at the ocean, water has always had places for life to work on it and benefit from it, but for centuries we've drained wetlands and simplified riparian areas. We need wildlife specialists, rewilding installations, and deep ecological understanding to restore the riparian areas and wetlands that used to sequester and store carbon and purify our water. You can create a thriving ecosystem of amazing edge effect between land and water that feeds people and heals the environment.
- **Wetland & Shore Restoration** - In many, perhaps most, areas, restoration needs to precede any farming activities. The waters are too toxic, the life too sparse, or the system too fragile to make a commercial profit yet, but the promise of what it can be will bring investors, restoration, and abundance. You can be the one to bring that change, set things in motion for a brighter future for all involved.
- **Artificial Reef Installations** - Design, plan, create, and install reefs to protect fragile new shore systems and provide habitat for an incredible diversity of life.

Education

- ***Pharmersea*** - Learn from ocean regenerative farming expert Dan Marquez who's consulted and worked with experts and ocean farming operations on both North American coasts. His vision encompasses the most complete regenerative plan for ocean restoration. Come learn from the best! Pharmersea.com
- ***Watershed Artisans*** - Craig Sponholtz and his team of watershed restoration and water harvesting experts are based in New Mexico, USA. They offer courses, workshops, professional training, consulting, installation, and restoration services - if you are interested in healing riparian areas, visit Watershed Artisans! WatershedArtisans.com
- ***Riparian Restoration Program*** - This Canadian program is hosted by Sustainability Resources in Alberta in conjunction with local and state government and commercial organizations. Their program has spread riparian restoration education and actively restored riparian areas since 2014 with hundreds of volunteers using native plants. SustainabilityResources.ca/resources/community-learning-events/riparian-restoration-conservation
- ***Statewide Riparian and Stream Ecosystem Education Programs in Texas*** - Involving a huge team of different riparian and educational institutions, this statewide program seeks to educate everyone on how to heal, manage, and read riparian landscapes.

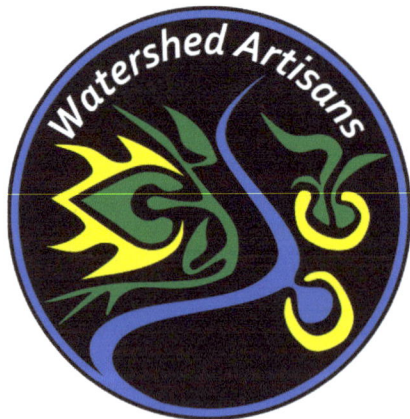

"The oceans are calling out for help! We believe restorative ocean farming is an intelligent solution for our Blue concerns. Ocean acidification is a clear sign that something must be done to mitigate human harm. Restorative ocean farming rebuilds marine biodiversity while revitalizing ecosystems. Kelp beds provide shelter and homes for many species; rebuilding our kelp forests is a vital step to healing our oceans.

Farming kelps makes me a Blue carbon farmer! Kelp sequesters carbon at ten times the rate of land-based plants. Kelp has unlimited applications, and America is just beginning to understand the many benefits and applications kelp has to offer. I believe it is time for local fresh sea vegetables to move onto American plates, personal care items, fertilizer, and fuel.

Seaweed farming is centuries old and a historic sustainable crop. It is just in the last few decades that the concept of ocean farming has come to America.

We have an opportunity to industrialize our oceans with responsible and sustainable practices that will help us transition gracefully into a Blue Economy!"

PharmerSea™

Dan Marquez

sea systems specialist and facilities expert, speaker,
AMA SeaBeauty co-founder, & co-founder of Pharmersea
Pharmersea.com

Large-Scale Design & Restoration

Want to terraform our world?

Can you imagine a completely different global landscape? Maybe it's just your area that you can visualize as regeneratively thriving, but do you feel called to make **big** changes? If you do, you need to follow that feeling. We need you to dive deep, to take that leap, and dream bigger than you thought possible. Your contribution could change the course of history, and that's no exaggeration. Already designers have changed entire generation's outlook and prospects in degraded areas all over the world. You can too. The tools, knowledge, and proven models are already in place - we just need courageous designers to create and inspire the world to embrace large-scale restoration.

Forget terraforming Mars - the earth needs you!

Careers

- *Ecological Civil Engineers* - We need our streets, parks, lights, and more to be rethought from an ecological perspective. Going beyond landscaping, this role will take traditional civil engineering into the regenerative space. Envision new cultural and behavioral patterns on a macro scale!

- *Large-Scale Land Restoration* - Green the manmade deserts, restore agricultural soils all over the world, and create resilient landscapes of plenty - you can be part of the global shift towards a syntropic system of abundance. We can reverse the desertification process by restoring and removing imbalance in the natural cycles and bringing back the biodiversity that once supported our world.

- *City Planning & Design* - Many of us have heard of China building cities of tomorrow without people even living in them yet: it's true, instead of adapting their current cities, they are building the future now to migrate into it. Many struggle with how to adapt our current systems to get us into the regenerative future, but it will take grand visions that disregard current limitations or perspectives to guide us out of these stormy waters. Make the city of your dreams real - it IS possible!

Regrarians.org 2017

Education

- **Sustainable Design Masterclass** - Neal Spackman and Raleigh Latham host a weekly webinar series that provides exclusive interviews and webinars with experts from all over the world in regeneration, focused on successful businesses and leading models. Learn from the cutting edge from the comfort of home! Subscribe & watch when they air live online or go back and rent past webinars on an individual basis - dive deep into their incredible library and learn from some of the best regenerative examples in the world!
- **Ecosystem Restoration Camps** - Sourcing volunteers from around the globe, this nonprofit organization is setting up camps of volunteer workers and volunteer expert designers who will create regenerative example sites all over the world. The first site is in Spain and work is currently underway - join the movement to demonstrate to the world what is possible! Show government agencies, non-governmental organizations, nonprofits, & humanitarian aid what we can do with the right tools and understanding. Let's go to camp! EcosystemRestorationCamps.org
- **REX Online** - Mentioned early, this online program taps into a wealth of knowledge through its network of experienced designers, many of whom have worked on large-scale restoration projects with governments and NGOs. If you are looking for a spectrum of professional experience in this arena, check out the REX! Rex.farm

ecosystem restoration camps

SUSTAINABLE DESIGN WEBINARS ON DEMAND

Regrarians.org

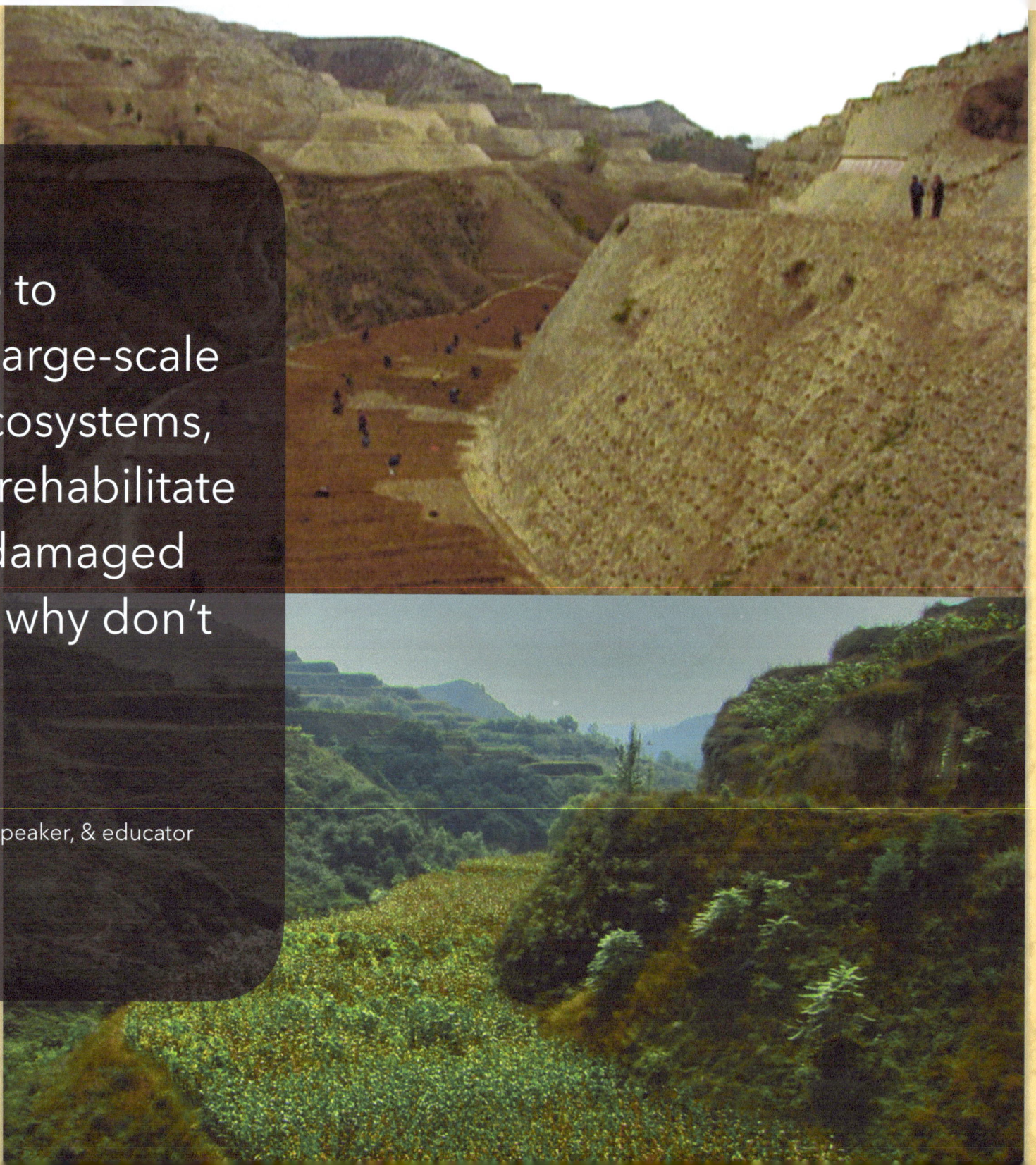

"It's possible to rehabilitate large-scale damaged ecosystems, so if we can rehabilitate large-scale damaged ecosystems, why don't we do that?"

John D. Liu
videographer, producer, speaker, & educator
EEMPC.org

Seed Farming & Plant Breeding

Do you LOVE seed saving or plant breeding?

Did you know that almost all the seeds sold are not grown by the company selling them? They source seed from giant seed houses and independent farmers all over the world. You often never know what climate your seed's parent plant grew in! Seed savers, home gardeners, and commercial farmers are all seeking locally adapted seeds, which opens up the possibility for bioregional and local seed libraries and companies everywhere!

Thirty years ago seed houses and companies didn't carry heirlooms in any great volume - the only remaining heirloom seed keepers were home gardeners, independent seed collectors, and plant breeders. Since that time there has been a renaissance of heirloom seeds and traditional farming methods (often termed organic or biodynamic), which has been facilitated by the ever growing demand for new varieties and more diversity from the public. They want new colors, tastes, and looks. This is also coinciding with the growing instability of conventional agriculture's methods and genetics, causing crop failures and market instability globally. Farmers are looking for resilient seed with adaptable genetic libraries of experience built into their genes by experience rather than questionable, costly, and narrow pre-programmed genetics, designed by scientists in a distant greenhouse. Farmers, families, and foodies alike are wanting their seeds and plants to be connected to the places they are consumed - they are all craving authenticity and connection that can only come through adaptation and localization.

Plant breeders and seed farmers who create the most resilient seeds will find top dollar for their germplasm. Brad Gates of Wild Boar Farms rewilded the tomato and in doing so has created an entirely new branch of the tomato family that is disease resistant, vigorous, pest resistant, more delicious, shockingly beautiful, diverse, and improved in overall nutritional value. He's created 60 varieties in 20 years, and his tomatoes are grown all over the world. Learn how to create new varieties - it's EASY: you can change our diet, world, and understanding of what's possible with a new plant or new branch to a plant family. You can make history with your seeds! Join the exciting cutting edge of food and seed where backyard breeders have long dominated as the leaders!

Careers

- *Regenerative Seed Farmer* - Regenerative farmers are needed to grow the seeds of tomorrow today. Seed saving is incredibly gratifying, and creating the most resilient adaptation of a variety is even more so. Be a seed grower & saver, supply the new regenerative farming movement from the ground up!
- *Regenerative Seed Company* - Help dozens of regenerative farmers sell their seeds by starting a seed company or partner with several growers and grow it all yourself - it's all possible!
- *Regenerative Plant Breeder* - More than tomatoes need to be rewilded - we need to breed back the diversity we've lost. Become a regenerative plant breeder and show what nature really can do!

Education

- *Native Seed Search* - This Southwestern USA organization preserves incredibly rare and sacred native seed, and they also offer workshops and trainings in seed saving and growing. Learn from a long cultural heritage of master plant breeders and seed savers. https://shop.nativeseeds.org
- *Seed Savers Exchange* - This organization is uniquely special: it connects US backyard seed savers in a cooperative that shares information and allows them to each sell their seeds without starting their own business. Find the rarest and well tended seed genetics, learn from their programs and workshops, and learn from the seed savers themselves as you connect through the network. Their book The Seed Garden is a superb reference manual for all levels of seed saver - learn how to save all varieties of seed with this beautiful and well written guide that every seed saver should own and cherish!
- *Seed Seva Seasonal Journey* - This is an online distance learning seed saving course through Sierra Seeds focused on indigenous techniques and permaculture. Learn from Rowen White, an inspirational and engaging teacher and expert seed saver, in a seven month immersion program starting April 2018.

"Seed saving has been conducted for at least 10,000 years. Our ancestors did it without fret or worry. The America's alone bear over 400 unique landraces of maize, hundreds upon hundreds of beans, thousands of oddly shaped and colorful and nutritious potatoes. Seeds founded our civilization. Diversity roared. From zebra striped lima beans, 30 foot tall and half dollar coin sized corn, wild cabbage, yellow skinned watermelons, neon green fleshed radishes - the world still gleams with seed diversity. But, it is we seed savers whom protect this diversity, their stories, education about their preservation, and the cultures they are associated it. As a seed saver we protect the ancestral labor and protect our food supply. We are stewards of seeds and their histories. Plant yourself as a seed saver with a local seed library, start your own garden and collection, talk with neighbors, talk with your elders. Learn and grow into a keeper of global food and seed diversity. WE are the future."

Stephen Smith author, heirloom seed preservationist, plant breeder, and educator.
SacredEagleSeeds.wixsite.com/sopi

Teaching & Consulting

Were you born to facilitate learning & help others find their path?

Passionate and professional regenerative teachers are needed all over the world today! If you love teaching but are stuck teaching subjects that don't further the regeneration or the progress of our culture, it's time for a change. The good news is you're already in demand. The public education system is trying its best to adapt to extremely trying circumstances, and there are many examples of schools testing radically different methods and even using permaculture to enhance their campus and educational experiences. These institutions sense permaculture and regenerative systems can provide what they are actually seeking: career paths that lead to lives of fulfillment and meaning for their students. Inevitably permaculture concepts and regenerative practices are going to find their way into the core of academia - the market demand for solutions to our economic stagnation and environmental degradation are too great.

You can teach children about permaculture and help them lead lives of joyful restoration and regeneration. You can educate professionals of all sorts of trades and niches in how regenerative practices can help re-skill and keep them competitive in the new regenerative economy. You can visit and teach those with the greatest needs in areas of distress all over the world. Teachers are needed everywhere at all levels.

Careers

- *Permaculture Teacher* - Teach the basic framework for all regenerative and holistic understanding - prepare and shape young minds and those unfamiliar with the three ethics and nature's patterns, systems, and principles. Help spread the lens through which all can see a brighter future!
- *Regenerative Agriculture & Horticulture Instructors* - Teach professional applications for regenerative concepts and help students find their way into rewarding and beneficial career paths.
- *Holistic Management Instructor* - Teach students how to use holistic management for life planning, business planning, site planning, cattle management, and decision-making.
- *NonViolent Communication Instructor* - Teach nonviolent communication. Help others learn to resolve conflicts quickly and positively. Help spread peace with your work as you empower individuals and communities to transcend their circumstances, the past, and their old patterns to become more compassionate, understood, giving, and free.
- *Site & Business Consultant* - Help businesses and land owners of all types become more regenerative or retrain their staff to adopt regenerative practices and ethical patterns. You can help retrain a staff in compassionate communication, waste management, project design and management, and so much more! These organizations need help transitioning, and you can be that facilitator!

Rhamis Kent 2016.

Education

- *NonViolent Communication Training* - Become a teacher of nonviolent communication or a conflict mitigator by learning with the Center for Nonviolent Communication. Help end violence and violent communication - help others and even entire communities learn to communicate with compassion. Cnvc.org/trainingcal
- *Holistic Management Certified Educator* - Get trained in holistic management in-depth. Become a teacher of holistic management and help others organize themselves, their business, or their farm or ranch, so they can plan their future with confidence. Holisticmanagement.org/ce-training-program/
- *Regenerative Entrepreneurs & Educators Online* - Learn best practices in education, marketing, speaking, presenting, classroom management, lesson design, entrepreneurship, business planning, and crowdfunding in an online, group coaching format. ThePermacultureStudent.com
- *Metta Certificate in NonViolence Studies* - Take a six month online program with the Metta Center for Nonviolence designed to teach learners the history, practical application, philosophy, core concepts, and key strategies of Nonviolence. Get connected to the Nonviolence community and start spreading peaceful resolution in your area. MettaCenter.org/research-education/metta-certificate-nonviolence-studies/

"We need more teachers now than ever in the history of the world, and we need them to teach the regenerative solutions to the greatest problems we've ever faced. We need you to join us in the movement to regenerate our world, our cultures, and our economies. The rewards waiting for us our beyond our imagination."

Matt Powers
author, heirloom seed farmer, homestead gardener, entrepreneur, and educator.
ThePermacultureStudent.com

Your Future, Our Future

Are you ready for a future of regenerative solutions & innovation?

It won't be farmers or engineers alone that will be transitioning into a new world, but all our industries and all their roles will change. Even as automation now is upending the job market, the regenerative economy will do so again but in reverse as many more people than those currently working will be needed to work hands-on with complex natural cycles and systems. Everyone is needed in this regenerative movement - the skills and understanding are accessible and adaptable to accommodate and include everyone. Not only that - this movement stands to benefit everyone as well. It's a win-win for everyone and everything.

It's important to note that all of these industries still need folks to sweep floors, clean bottles, recycle/upcycle/compost materials, and deliver products locally and online - there'll be a lot of new jobs at all levels opening up as these new companies and industries come online. It should be noted that many of these career paths rely or are enhanced by a four year college degree, masters, or even a Phd. The paths in this guide are not mutually exclusive - instead they all can enhance each other and many can be combined even though they are presented as separate career paths in this guide: you can work with cattle, fungi, rare seeds, teach, and consult! There's no limit to what you can do with regenerative systems and your life - there are so many connections that can be made to create an abundance, spread compassion, restore the environment, meet incredible like-minded people, and prepare wisely for the future.

We need everyone to populate this economy; there is no lack of jobs in the regenerative space. The future holds an economy of abundance - this is your invitation!

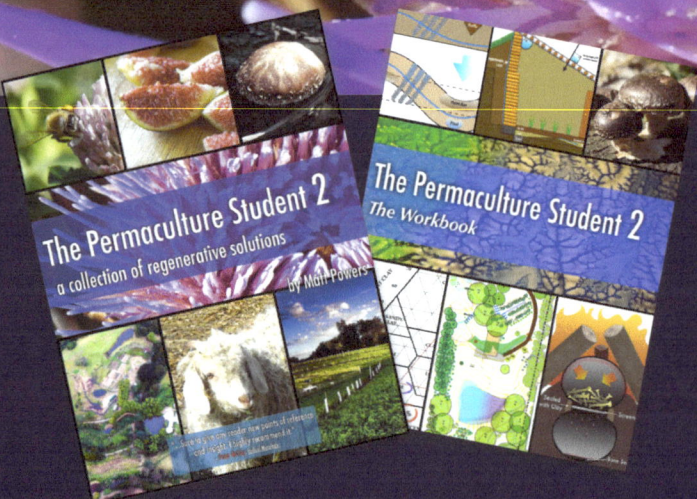

About the Author

Matt Powers is a gardener, seed saver, plant breeder, author, educator, and entrepreneur who teaches people all over the world how to live more regeneratively through online courses, videos, podcasts, and books. In 2015, Matt left teaching teachers best practices and public high school students 10th grade English and music production to teach permaculture online, write books, and speak at universities, schools, and conferences all over the American West & Midwest when he wrote and crowdfunded the printing of The Permaculture Student 1 - the first of five books released in the past two years by Matt. Translations of his books are available in Spanish, Polish, and Arabic with French, Swahili, Russian, and Italian coming soon.

Matt provides daily inspirational and motivational content online and is one of the most-followed permaculture teachers online with over 30,000 Twitter followers and tens of thousands of followers in his many Facebook groups and pages ranging in topics from permaculture education to entrepreneurship to gardening to fungi and more. Matt lives with his family in Washington State outside Seattle currently.

Listen to Matt on An Abundant Future on iTunes or Soundcloud.com/AbundantFuture

Order Matt's books & enroll in his courses online at ThePermacultureStudent.com

Matt's books are also available on Amazon, Barnes&Noble, your local library, and your local book store by request.

Natural Capital™

Plant Database

permacultureplantdata.com

Custom plant lists for your climate, soils, and ecological design solutions.

For tropics, dry lands and cold climates.   *Over 4000 users in 70 countries.*

The Natural Capital™ Plant Database is the first designer focused plant information and an educational resource for ecological design. The focus of this resource is to help gardeners, homesteaders, and permaculture designers build plant relationships, create natural capital, and enhance ecological services.

Our designers have combined the best sources of plant research and documentation to provide the highest integrity of detail. The database provides characteristics, tolerances and behaviors, ecological functions, human uses, concerns, and plant associates. It encourages polyculture design so that each plant may thrive in its most desireable environment, supply a niche function, support ecological functions for the ecology, and provide harvests for the occupants.

Free memberships enable access to all plant list data.
Individual subsriptions enable searching for plants suited to site conditions .
Designer subscriptions enable search access and a spreadsheet download.

visit **permacultureplantdata.com** to learn more

www.ingramcontent.com/pod-product-compliance
Lightning Source LLC
Chambersburg PA
CBHW041552030426

42336CB00004B/52